DEVOTIONS FOR RUNNERS

INSPIRED LIVING SERIES

DEVOTIONS FOR RUNNERS

BY

CECIL MURPHEY

New York Times Bestselling Author

eISBN: 978-1-937776-15-2
ISBN 13: 978-1-937776-88-6

OTHER BOOKS BY CECIL MURPHEY

Inspired Living Devotional Series:

Devotions for Couples
Devotions for Dieters
Devotions for Runners
Revitalize Your Prayer Life: Inspired
Living Series Companion

More Titles:

90 Minutes in Heaven (with Don Piper)
Gifted Hands: The Ben Carson
Story (with Dr. Ben Carson)
Rebel with a Cause (with Franklin Graham)
Because You Care: Spiritual Encouragement for
Caregivers (by Cecil Murphey and Twila Belk)
When Someone You Love No Longer Remembers
The Spirit of Christmas (by Cecil
Murphey and Marley Gibson)
Unleash the Writer Within
Knowing God, Knowing Myself
When a Man You Love Was Abused
When God Turned Off the Lights

A NEW FOREWORD

I love to run. No other exercise or sport stimulates me the same way. That's why I've hit the pavement for more than 35 years and I'm still going at it. I'm slower and I've cut down on the number of miles, but I can't think of my life without running.

I'm also a runner and not a jogger.

When I wrote this book 30 years ago, the editorial staff preferred the term, *jogging*. I liked the word *running*.

There *is* a difference and this isn't to say that one is better than the other. Jogging refers to a slower, more leisurely pace and someone called it trotting. It's less stressful and easier on the body; running refers to a faster pace and requires more effort. For many people, running at a fast pace on hard surfaces eventually ruins their knees. I've been blessed because my knees are fine.

The publisher insisted on jogging because they wanted me to encourage physical movement, not a fast pace. They were probably right. Jogging is a nice, easy exercise with the body in action.

I prefer the faster-paced form and that fits with me and with my lifestyle. When I lived in Kenya, one of the names the Africans gave me was Haraka—quick or fast. That expresses who I am.

I don't see running as an issue about speed (although some people make it that way), but it's about caring for our bodies, God's holy temple. Paul exhorts us to give our bodies to God as living sacrifices. (See Romans 12:1.) One of the first rules of caring for bodies is to exercise them.

For most people, jogging is a better exercise and they can keep it going years longer. As I wrote above, I've been a runner for more than 35 years and there aren't that many still out there doing it after that length of time. Not only do their knees give out, but their joints ache, and they say with sadness, "I used to run, but . . ."

Some runners are able to persist by running on the tracks around local schools because they're so well insulated, which causes less stress on the skeletal frame.

By contrast, the joggers seem able to keep up the habit with less body exertion. So if you're just beginning or thinking seriously about running, I suggest you focus on jogging. Enjoy the less stressful form of body movement.

Regardless, move that body. If you keep it going now, it will keep you going later.

I PROBABLY OUGHT TO DO SOMETHING ABOUT IT

So whether you eat or drink, or whatever you do, do it all for the glory of God. (1 Corinthians 10:31)

Week 1, Day 1

Dr. Morgan entered the room carrying a manila folder under his arm. He laid the folder on the table and read the paper clipped to the top. He glanced up at me and smiled. "Basically, you're in pretty good shape." Then he paused.

"But?"

"Your blood pressure's on the high side of the normal range," he said. "Not an immediate concern—"

"But could be a problem in the future?"

He nodded. "For right now we'll watch it and see what happens."

As I left the doctor's office and drove home, I thought of the prognosis. Both my parents, as well as my brothers and sisters, already fight with high blood pressure. *I probably ought to do something about it,* I said to myself.

A few days later in my devotional time I came across the Apostle Paul's words in 1 Corinthians.

3

Those words, along with reading I had been doing on high blood pressure and physical fitness, convinced me that I not only needed to do something—I would.

I joined a health spa and started out on a regular program. I was on my way toward the immediate goal of lowering my blood pressure. My reading told me that reduced weight and physical exercise were the two best solutions, especially in instances like mine where the problem had not reached dangerous proportions.

Every once in a while I'd start to let up and then 1 Corinthians 10:31 would pop into my mind. That verse tormented me for at least four years.

In the twenty years that I have been a Christian, no other Scripture has troubled me like this one. I also knew long ago that obedience to the *principle* of 1 Corinthians would drastically alter my life-style. It would force me to pray and to think more seriously about my behavior. Most of all, it meant my eating would come under God's scrutiny. "So, whether you eat or drink, or whatever you do, do all to the glory of God."

Laying that verse beside two other statements in 1 Corinthians (3:16 and 6:19) which state that the body is God's holy temple only increased my discomfort. As I remember that my body belongs to God, which he calls a holy temple, then I have to bring my eating and all my activities into line.

In my early Christian days I did not think God cared much about how I treated my body. His interest lay primarily in the spiritual aspects—my prayers, Bible reading, giving, church fellowship, and service.

Over the years I largely ignored 1 Corinthians 10:31. Sometimes it would occur to me and I'd cut down on my eating, do away with rich desserts, or walk half a block for exercise. Then I would forget about the Corinthians passage again. But after my visit to Dr. Morgan, I couldn't ignore it any longer.

"All right, Lord," I said, "I'll begin putting that verse into practice."

I started in the food department. It meant changing my eating style. I read about nutrition and cut out products of little or questionable value, such as sugar and white flour. I checked my weight regularly. Although no one ever categorized me as obese, the pounds were clinging to me. My middle years spread mostly around my middle in a three-inch overlap above my belt.

We made gradual changes—simpler meals and more raw foods. We concerned ourselves with balanced meals.

Exercise became the next step. "...or whatever you do...."

I had never been interested in team sports and had excused myself by saying, "I'm not the athletic type." I tried calisthenics for a few weeks, grew bored, and stopped.

Then I tried running. And I got hooked.

Today I can't boast, "See, Lord, I'm doing everything to your glory," but I can say, "Lord, I'm getting closer."

Running began as my response to my doctor's report and a single verse from the New Testament. I have since developed other reasons for running, but initially it came about as an act of obedience.

At my last physical exam, when the nurse took my pulse and blood pressure she looked at the figures and checked again. "Do you jog?" she asked.

"Sure do," I said, smiling.

"Guess that accounts for the low figures," she said and marked them on her chart.

I felt a real high as I left the doctor that morning—so different from the experience four years earlier. And since then I've learned more about faithfulness in being a good caretaker of God's temple.

Lord God, remind me of 1 Corinthians 10:31 as often as I need it. I easily forget that this body of mine is your temple. Help me glorify you in everything. Amen.

THE RUNNER'S COST

And if you do not carry your own cross and follow me, you cannot be my disciple. But don't begin until you count the cost. For who would begin construction of a building without first calculating the cost to see if there is enough money to finish it? Otherwise, you might complete only the foundation before running out of money, and then everyone would laugh at you. They would say, 'There's the person who started that building and couldn't afford to finish it!' (Luke 14:27–30)

Week 1, Day 2

The idea had been nagging at me for weeks. Everywhere I went I saw joggers, read about marathons, or heard someone talking about finishing a 10K race. It was like a foreign language, but it also intrigued me.

I had started a physical program two years earlier and had dropped off nearly twenty-five pounds by carefully watching my weight and exercising at a local spa. I spent twenty minutes three times weekly on the treadmill. That provided my only taste of running.

Yet I hesitated. I didn't want to get involved in running and then give it up in three months. If I decided to run, it would become a lifetime commitment for me.

I went to the library and checked out a book on running, picked up a couple of books in a bookstore, saw running magazines at a newsstand and bought one, subscribed to it, and read it eagerly. All of this occurred before I ever ran. I wanted to know about the physical benefits, but just as much I needed to comprehend the negative side.

Shirley, my wife, and I talked about it. I didn't want to start running alone. I was self-conscious enough that I didn't want to get out there on the streets, feeling awkward to begin with, and sensing the stares of people passing by in their automobiles.

We psyched ourselves up, reminding ourselves that running is one of the top, all-around physical exercises, and especially good for the cardiovascular system.

We finally decided to try, making a mental commitment to run at least a full month before quitting. We also decided to do our running at 5:30 A.M., before our neighbors got up.

Next we drove up the street and, using the odometer of our car, mentally marked off every stretch of the road in tenths.

"Let's shoot for half a mile," I said.

Shirley agreed and added, "Without walking."

We made the half mile. From there we graduated to six-tenths and eventually to a whole mile.

In planning to accomplish that first mile, we realized two things. First, we had counted the cost. A commitment to running would entail time—at least three times a week. We expected that eventually we would spend thirty minutes each time. We didn't know how we'd squeeze in that much running, but we decided it would take priority.

Second, I viewed this undertaking as more than a physical exercise. It was part of my determination to offer my body as a living sacrifice to Jesus Christ, as the Apostle Paul exhorts in Romans 12:1.

That meant that as I became more physically fit, I actually pleased God. No way to lose on that one.

The experts in the running field assured me of great benefits. I got rid of another five pounds of flab. But even better, my blood pressure, which had hovered just below the danger line, soon rested in the comfortable average range. Running increased my lung capacity and stirred up my cardiovascular systems for greater efficiency. I felt better about myself—not only looking better, but feeling better.

In thinking it all over, I'm glad I'm a runner. And in counting costs and weighing the benefits, I discovered one other benefit most of the writers don't mention. I feel a closeness with Jesus Christ when I run. Perhaps it's being part of nature, gliding past the trees, seeing the grass wave gently in the wind or feeling the sun rays warming my already perspiring body.

Even counting the negative costs of sore legs, aches and calluses, the setting aside of time, I'm glad I'm a runner.

Lord, help me be a faithful runner and a faithful Christian—whatever it costs. Amen.

SETTING YOUR GOAL

I have fought the good fight, I have finished the race, and I have remained faithful. (2 Timothy 4:7)

Week 1, Day 3

My breath came in short gasps, my body weakened, and I felt myself ready to stumble. I lurched slightly forward, not sure if I could make it. I turned my face to my wife and asked, "How you doing?"

"Okay," she said. The wrong answer. I hoped she'd say, "Let's quit." She looked every bit as weak as I felt, but she kept moving forward and gave no indication of quitting.

I straightened slightly, gritted my teeth, and raced on, reminding myself that the agony would not last forever.

The telephone pole loomed ahead—it marked the end of our run. Seeing the end so close, I spurted ahead with a final burst of energy I didn't know I had. I reached the spot a full two seconds before Shirley.

I leaned against the pole, taking deep gulps of air, trying to ignore the searing pain of my lungs. I wanted to collapse on the ground but feared that if I did, I might not get up again.

"We made it," Shirley said between gasps.

I nodded, not wanting to waste any of my precious oxygen in speaking. Then her words hit me. *We had made it!* A euphoric wave engulfed me.

I grinned. "Hey, we did make it!"

We had set our goal, stuck it out, and completed the course. *One full mile.*

A mile doesn't sound like much to anyone who runs regularly. But for two people who had recently begun to exercise, it was an accomplishment.

That euphoric feeling stayed with me all morning. Even back home in the shower, I felt as though winning an Olympic medal could not have given a greater sense of satisfaction.

I felt a little like what the Apostle Paul might have felt when he wrote his last words to Timothy: I have fought the good fight, I have finished the race, and I have remained faithful. (2 Timothy 4:7)

For me as a Christian and as a runner, I'm always facing new goals. And when I reach them, I find myself rejoicing. I hope that when it comes to the end of my life I can echo the words of the famed apostle, "I have finished the race."

Loving Father, keep me setting new goals until I complete my final course. Amen.

Keeping It Off

Don't you realize that your body is the temple of the Holy Spirit, who lives in you and was given to you by God? You do not belong to yourself, for God bought you with a high price. So you must honor God with your body. (1 Corinthians 6:19–20)

Week 1, Day 4

Many people can lose weight. They often don't keep it off. One reason they ultimately fail is that they try by diet alone. The ideal weight program balances diet along with exercise. My friend Jimmy, a trim 170 at just under six feet, says that as long as he runs twenty-five miles a week he doesn't have to think about his weight. He's been running those miles for years.

Losing weight is important, not only because of how people look to others. Thinner bodies give them more confidence and assurance. It also pleases God. "What? You didn't know that the body is the temple of the Holy Spirit?" He's saying to the people at Corinth (Their problem wasn't being overweight, but it did affect the body), "Your body is sacred. It's God's dwelling place."

Then he adds, "So glorify God in your body."

What an incentive for running: trimming up and shaping up this wonderful temple which God inhabits. The trimmer and shapelier Christians become, the more they please God by the way they take care of his special house.

God, strengthen my desire to glorify you in my body. Amen.

MAKING CHANGES

And I am certain that God, who began the good work within you, will continue his work until it is finally finished on the day when Christ Jesus returns. (Philippians 1:6)

Week 1, Day 5

Dan joined a weight-watchers group six years ago to lose forty pounds. He succeeded. He lost the weight and weighed in at a slim 170 on his slightly more six-foot frame. Almost as soon as he reached his goal, Dan stopped watching his caloric intake. Pound by pound the scales sneaked back up toward the 230 mark. Dan has never learned that proper nutrition is a lifetime commitment. It means a change of life-style.

It works that way in every realm of life. In running, too. Many people start the sport with enthusiasm. They buy shoes, hand-initialed warm-up suits, matching shirts and shorts. They get out there and tear up the track. Yet within a year they have dropped out. They drop out because they don't enter into running with a lifetime commitment.

Five years and thirty pounds ago I changed my lifestyle. I read everything I could about how to achieve permanent weight loss. When I started the slim-down program, augmented by exercise, I also committed myself to find a style of eating that I could maintain the rest of my life. I knew that holding my weight down might prove even harder than getting it there in the first place.

Whenever I make any change that's permanent, it takes a mind-set to accomplish. I have to convince myself that I'm committing myself for life.

That's the kind of commitment God makes. The Apostle Paul assures us that once God begins to work in us, he continues until the day of Jesus Christ. By that the apostle means until the Second Coming, until the end of time.

God, you committed yourself to me. Remind me that you'll never stop or turn from me. Amen.

THE NEW ME

Anyone who belongs to Christ has become a new person. The old life is gone; a new life has begun! (2 Corinthians 5:17)

Week 1, Day 6

After my conversion at age twenty-one, life took on a new meaning. Almost everything changed. I experienced some drastic changes in behavior: I cleaned up my language, got rid of bad habits. Other parts of my life changed more slowly, but nonetheless the new life had started.

I was in the navy at the time. I remember several months after my encounter with Jesus Christ, a WAVE who worked in the same office said to me, "I don't know what's happened to you, but you're different lately." She indicated she liked the difference. So did I.

My experience began at age twenty-one. It still goes on. I am never a finished product. I am always "becoming" a new person—never quite arrived, but always in the process.

I was thinking of that this evening after a leisurely paced eight-mile run. I am a different person because of my relationship with Christ. As I thought of that, I realized that even my body is different.

I weigh less. I have better muscle tone. I feel better. My heart has become a more efficient pump. The kidneys carry off biochemical waste products. The liver fires up its enzyme system to help purify the blood and replace enzymes used in running. When I get into long-distance running, fat cells turn their fat into the blood stream and burn up as energy. Running stimulates the entire metabolic process of the body.

My brain, because of new loads of oxygen, is recharged when I run. This may explain why creative ideas float through the minds of runners. We're in the midst of a high—a well-being—because our bodies are at their best and are renewing themselves.

Some researchers claim that running actually enables people to live longer. There's no documented proof of that. I believe that runners have a higher level *quality* of living, in the same way that I believe Christians have a higher quality of life than nonbelievers.

I want to be a healthy mind in a healthy body. I yearn to be a completely new person in a healthy body. Nothing reaches that final stage until the resurrection. But, like the Apostle Paul, I train myself for the event. I strive forward, reminding myself that "the old has passed away, behold, the new has come."

Loving Savior, I am becoming not only a new person, but a better person. Knowing your love is what makes me better. Amen.

EASY ANSWERS

We must suffer many hardships to enter the Kingdom of God. (Acts 14:22)

Week 1, Day 7

People always search for easy answers. Runners prove no exception. Use bee pollen for increased energy. Brand R shoe gives you extra speed. Drink Alka-aid for stamina. Don't forget lightweight shorts which give you a few seconds' edge on others.

The trouble with all the magic formulas and the special gear is that they really don't help—at least not much. There are no easy answers to running fast or long. There are no easy answers to anything significant or important in life.

The top runners become top runners out of determination, right training, and a commitment to the sport. They also have natural ability. But natural ability alone won't do it. Neither do they win or lose the race because of wearing a particular style of jogging shorts or red shoes instead of blue and white ones. All good athletes know that success comes from hard work, dedication, and know-how.

This is like the young man who came to Jesus, asking what to do to inherit eternal life. He wanted an easy answer. When Jesus said "Keep the commandments," he hurriedly replied that he had kept them all.

Jesus said, "Sell what you have and give to the poor." That was no easy answer. Jesus demanded total commitment, an all-out effort. The young man departed, sorrowing, because he was wealthy. He didn't want to get rid of his wealth. He only wanted an easy solution to keep all his bounty and get the blessings of God besides.

Most people who want easy answers really say that they don't want to persevere or work hard for the results. But life just doesn't work that way. Singers practice hours each day. A young ballerina I know spends most of her nonschool hours practicing, working, and training, so that one day she'll not only be professional, but she'll be a top ballerina. No easy answers for that young lady. She's paying the price by hard work and commitment.

So it doesn't matter whether we're talking about running, learning a language, moving ahead in our jobs, or progressing in God's kingdom. It's still the same: no easy answers.

Holy God, teach me that nothing of real value comes easily. Help me realize that running for Jesus involves total commitment of myself. Amen.

WARMING UP

It is good to give thanks to the LORD, to sing praises to the Most High. It is good to proclaim your unfailing love in the morning, your faithfulness in the evening. (Psalm 92:1, 2)

Week 2, Day 1

Any time you see a horde of people preparing to do a 5K (3.1 miles) or 10K (6.3 miles) run, you can always depend on seeing them involved in one thing: warming up. Some run half a mile to limber up. Others stretch, often putting themselves in strange positions. You might notice a few doing calisthenics. They all warm up for a purpose.

The experts have been exhorting for years, "Warm up to avoid injury." Those who run longer distances especially need to heed this advice. After people run for a while (particularly those who average thirty or more miles weekly), they develop tight muscles in the back of their legs.

Tests indicate that runners who begin without first warming up have abnormal EKG, and it takes time for this to stabilize. The heart needs warm-up time for the coronary arteries to dilate, allowing more blood to flow through them. The warm-up gets the heart rate up, but it also relaxes and stretches those tense muscles.

When I think of the spiritual dimension of life, I wonder how many Christians value the importance of warming up, the need to stretch muscles of the soul before starting out the day.

Many Christians jump out of bed (or crawl, according to their temperament) and run head-long into the activities of the day. Then they often question, "Why do I feel so tense?" They wonder why they worry or why the day has gone sour by mid afternoon.

Growing as a Christian requires the same diligence as any sport. The Bible *assumes* prayer as a daily commitment, rather than exhorting us to do it. Take the Psalms, for instance. Psalms 5:3 says, "Each morning I bring my requests to you and wait expectantly." Or O Lord, I cry out to you. I will keep on pleading day by day (Psalm 88:13).

The Apostle Paul writes, Don't worry about anything; instead, pray about everything. Tell God what you need, and thank him for all he has done" (Philippians 4:6). Mark says of Jesus, "Before day-break the next morning, Jesus got up and went out to an isolated place to pray" (Mark 1:35).

If, as the physical experts tell us, inadequate warm-up causes all kinds of troubles, from shin splints to inflammation of the Achilles tendon, then runners need to listen. And they do! Yet they tend to take the need for a soul warm-up loosely.

Tomorrow morning, how about a chapter from the Bible before you really start the day? A few minutes of prayer? At least warm up with God's fellowship before you start the day.

Dear Father, teach me to start today (and every day) with you. Amen.

SIDE STITCHES

And athletes cannot win the prize unless they follow the rules. (2 Timothy 2:5)

Week 2, Day 2

About the middle of the second mile it hit me—a side stitch.

Not a great pain, just a jabbing little nuisance. At first I decided to ignore it. It did not lessen. I remembered the folk remedies from boyhood days. I used to hold my right hand with my thumb inside for thirty seconds. I don't remember if it ever helped before or not, but everyone in our neighborhood swore that was the only thing to do.

It didn't help me during the race.

Actually a side stitch is a normal physical phenomenon. It almost always occurs when you're running hard enough to breathe deeply for a long time. Some runners are more susceptible than others.

The permanent help for side stitches is training. People in good condition rarely get a side stitch. As a runner's fitness increases, the side stitch either disappears completely or occurs less frequently and with less intensity.

I later learned the one method of getting rid of the side stitch: *slow down*. You don't have to stop; merely decrease your pace, and breathe deeply, using your stomach muscles.

In that race, I came to a walk for the next half-mile, not because I knew to do that, but because I couldn't run anymore. The stitch disappeared, and I took off again. When I reached the finish line, my time was slower than I had hoped. But no stitch troubled me.

It seems to me that at times in life I behave exactly as I did in that race. I charge ahead, running pell-mell, and, whammo, I'm stopped.

I'm learning that when I forge ahead, leaving the Lord behind by my neglect, he has all kinds of ways of stopping me. Once I realize what has happened, I slow down to reassess the situation; and while I move forward, I do it cautiously. I've had too many spiritual side stitches from outrunning the leading of the Holy Spirit. I pray, "Lord, help me slow down. I want to move by your direction."

The Apostle Paul refers to races of his day. If racers did not follow the rules, the judges disqualified them. He exhorts us to do things the right way. And the right way, of course, is God's way.

With his help, I'm overcoming those blocks and setbacks, being more sensitive to the leading of the Holy Spirit. Sometimes I even find myself singing,

"Where he leads, I will follow...." And I mean it, too.

Lord Jesus, help me not to run ahead of you today. Make me more sensitive to your Holy Spirit. Amen.

THE UPPER HALF

The body has many different parts, not just one part. All of you together are Christ's body, and each of you is a part of it. (1 Corinthians 12:14, 27)

Week 2, Day 3

Top runners know that for better results they can't concentrate only on arms and legs. They also know they need exercise for the upper half. On nonrunning days, they suggest that people exercise the biceps, upper arms, stomachs, abdomen and hips. There's good evidence that those who give equal time to the other muscles recover faster from hard runs. Their bodies tend to be in better all-around health. Just holding the arms at ninety-degree angles or finding extra leg power in those last few miles requires added muscular strength.

One form of exercising those muscles is through weight lifting. But a word of caution. Here's the rule about weights: heavy weights and many repetitions build strength *and* bulky bodies. Light weights and many repetitions build stamina and a lean body. This applies to both men and women. Exercising the upper half is for firming up the body, not adding bulky muscles.

When I stopped to think about all-around exercise, it made sense. Now I'm exercising on nonrunning days for the rest of me, especially the upper half. I recognize that every part of my body is important, important because God created it.

Exercising the entire body reminds me of the Apostle Paul's understanding of the church. For him, each person is like one part of that body. "The body has many different parts, not just one part." (1 Corinthians 12:14). He writes in the Corinthian letter that one part's being small or not particularly attractive does not make it less essential. He emphasized that we need every part to have a complete body.

It's not enough to acknowledge that each part belongs. Each also has a function. Only when each part performs as nature intended is the body at its best.

Each muscle needs exercising. In the same way that we try to tone up our muscles over the entire body in exercise, we don't want to limit the body of Christ (the church) to a few, such as the pastors, teachers, and elders.

It's another way of saying that whatever gifts we have, we use them for the edifying of the entire body. And God gives gifts to every one of us "… so we can help each other" (1 Corinthians 12:7).

God, remind me today to care for my entire body. Help me also to remember that I'm part of your body, the church. Amen.

BEAUTIFUL FEET

Stand your ground . . . .For shoes, put on the peace that comes from the Good News . . . (Ephesians 6:14–15)

Week 2, Day 4

I sat on the front steps with my daughter, Cecile, while we both put on our running shoes. I stared at my bare feet: calluses on the big toe, a blood blister on the left foot where my shoes rubbed. Yet as I surveyed them, they looked like a runner's feet. I remembered staring at my legs after my morning shower and thinking, *They're beginning to look like a runner's legs.* My family had kidded me for at least three years because I had no bulging calf muscles. But my legs had gradually changed in shape—not only the calf muscles showed but there was no trace of flab anywhere.

As she saw me staring at my feet, Cecile said, as if reading my mind, "Your legs make you look like a runner. There's a beautiful shape to them."

Then I thought of the verse in Isaiah which says, "How beautiful on the mountains are the feet of the messenger who brings good news, the good news of peace . . ." (Isaiah 52:7).

Immediately a picture flashed into my mind. In the biblical days and long before rapid forms of communication such as phones and telegraphs, runners carried important messages from town to town. Often the king awaited news from battle, and a messenger ran across the plains to deliver the word of victory or defeat.

I envisioned myself as the one running, surging over the hills and valleys of Palestine, skipping over rocks and speeding up over the grassy plain. Nothing slowed me down. As I approached a village, I yelled, "Good news!" Crowds formed along the road as I passed. With only the barest decrease in speed, I yelled out, "Good news! God loves you! Jesus Christ died for you! Live forever!" The crowds cheered as I disappeared from view.

Then I looked down at my slightly misshapen feet again. To a nonrunner, there's nothing attractive about calluses. To me, they were beautiful. They bore the marks of running up and down hills and across paved roads. Maybe I wasn't yelling the good news of love as I ran. But in my heart the sense of God's presence and God's love was there.

Not only are my feet beautiful. I'm beautiful all over—and so are you—because we're his creation.

Loving God, thank you that I am beautiful—every part of me. Amen.

TRAINING THE HEART

*God blesses those whose hearts are pure, for they will see God.
(Matthew 5:8)*

Week 2, Day 5

My heart is probably bigger than that of the average American. I certainly know it's in better condition. How about yours? One way to find out is to check your pulse. The average adult's heart beats about seventy-five times a minute. Those of us who exercise regularly have figures as low as the fifties. A good heart beats slower and takes longer to wear out.

The way to get that heart working at its best is to exercise it. This muscle requires sports vigorous enough to raise the pulse to at least 120 beats a minute and sustain it for a minimum of half an hour.

The best sports to train the heart are running, swimming, cycling, skating, cross-country skiing, jumping, and rowing. These are the continuous and rhythmic sports. Others, such as golf, weight lifting, and tennis are not usually vigorous enough. When most people play tennis, they spend 80 percent of their time standing around waiting for the ball, and they seldom get their pulses up to the 120 beats, much less keep it there for an extended period.

In recent years, doctors have pushed their heart patients into physical exercise. One man, who had never exercised in his life except during required physical fitness courses in school, found himself taking two-mile runs every morning. His doctor tells him that his heart is better now than it's been in twenty years, even though he's had heart surgery twice. He said, "I wish someone had told me about exercise before."

It works like this: With continued exercise, the heart muscle becomes larger and stronger. This results in pumping more blood with each beat and therefore it doesn't need to beat as often.

It's the heart that keeps us fit. It's also interesting that when we speak of love, of the place of the affections, we also talk of the heart. Many ancient cultures, including the Jews, believed that this large muscle was the source of all our emotions.

Perhaps that's why the Bible speaks so much about the heart. Not the literal muscle, of course. The biblical writers use the word referring to the center of our being. We're told to keep our hearts pure, to set our hearts on things above. Where our treasures are, our hearts are, too.

Whether we're talking about physical well-being or spiritual health, we need both as God's people. As we exercise *both* our hearts, we grow stronger and healthier.

Lord of life, train my heart that I might always want you more than anything else in life. Amen.

SLEEP

It is useless for you to work so hard from early morning until late at night, anxiously working for food to eat; for God gives rest to his loved ones. (Psalm 127:2)

Week 2, Day 6

For half of my life I hated the idea of sleep. It prevented me from continuing with my activities. It stopped the creative flow. I can remember during my twenties and even until my midthirties when I found ways to fight off sleep. I seldom slept more than five hours at a time.

Nowadays researchers tell us about the rejuvenation from sleep. As I've read the literature, it makes me more comfortable giving in at night to weariness.

Why this need for sleep anyway? We know we run out of energy, which is the way our bodies speak to us. The maintenance department goes to work once we close up for the night. Of special interest to runners is what researchers call slow-wave sleep. That's when the growth hormone in the body promotes protein synthesis, to repair the worn-out cells from the day's activities.

While results are not conclusive, research indicates that runners get a higher share of slow-wave sleep than sedentary people. That is, the active types get more quality sleep than unfit individuals. This is especially true on nights after hard exercise.

Sedentary types often complain of lack of sleep and frequent disturbances during the night. But runners, especially the serious ones who see themselves as caregivers of God's holy temple, know the benefits of a good night's rest. They also know the pleasure of awakening in the morning, refreshed and ready to tackle the new day.

I can't think of a more marvelous idea than, upon awakening and appreciating the rest of the night, to say, "He gives to his beloved sleep."

I awakened this morning after a nine-mile run yesterday. I lay in bed, adjusting myself to the newness of the day. Birds chirped outside my window, greeting the first rays of daylight. I sighed. "Thanks, God, for a goodnight's rest." I also thanked him because he gave me, one of his beloved, sleep.

Our Father, thank you for the gift of sleep. May I always enjoy rest as I remember your love for me. Amen.

Beautiful LSD

"Listen! A farmer went out to plant some seed. As he scattered it across his field, some of the seed fell on a footpath, and the birds came and ate it. Other seed fell on shallow soil with underlying rock. The seed sprouted quickly because the soil was shallow. But the plant soon wilted under the hot sun, and since it didn't have deep roots, it died. Other seed fell among thorns that grew up and choked out the tender plants so they produced no grain. Still other seeds fell on fertile soil, and they sprouted, grew, and produced a crop that was thirty, sixty, and even a hundred times as much as had been planted!" (Mark 4:3-8)

Week 2, Day 7

Want to know a secret? If there's any secret I can share with you about running, it's LSD. You know why it's a secret? Because either most people don't know—or they don't believe it.

LSD, translated into runner's jargon by Joe Henderson, means *long, slow distance.* He means simply that when you're going to run long distances (and for him *long distance* stands for anything up to fifty miles), don't throw all your energy into the first

35

two miles. He suggests that you pace yourself, taking it slow. This method takes longer to reach the destination—*but* the runner gets there without dropping out at midpoint.

I don't run fifty miles a day. I've never run fifty in a week. But I've learned to apply Henderson's term to practical usage.

I learned the secret quite by accident. Jim and I run together every Wednesday for five or six miles. Originally we tried eight together. We either stopped short or came back exhausted. I also realized that on Tuesdays I take a long run, often twelve miles. When I'd run with Jim the following day, I wouldn't have the stamina for another long, hard run. We cut our distance down to five miles.

We enjoyed each other and talked as we ran; so we slowed down. Occasionally we'd become so engrossed in our conversation, we'd change to a fast walk. We discovered that because we didn't push ourselves for time, we finished the day's course refreshed.

And haven't we all seen this in the church too? Some converts hear the Gospel, respond, and within six months they involve themselves in every conceivable activity. However, by the end of the first year, they have burned out and no one ever hears from them again.

Others start out all right, but never quite make it because they have too many demands calling them aside. Worries, burdens, and problems, overwhelm them, and they drop out.

We all know the fruitful kind. They're steady and dependable. You never have to ask, "Will Fred be here?" You know he will.

Jesus talked about people like those I've described above. He did it in a parable about a farmer who went out and planted seed. A few seeds never even got started. Some fell on rocky ground and, not having much stamina (soil), sprang up into life; but when it got hot, those plants died away. Other seeds bedded among thorns which choked them. Jesus also told about a fourth kind of seed— the fruitful. They endured, ". . . and produced a crop that was thirty, sixty, and even a hundred times as much as had been planted!" (Mark 4:8).

It works the same with running. LSD—that's the secret.

Lord, don't let me get caught up in such fast-paced living that I wear out. Remind me of LSD for more fruitfulness. Amen.

TIRED-OUT DAYS

*He gives power to the weak and strength to the powerless.
(Isaiah 40:29)*

Week 3, Day 1

By the time I had completed the second mile, my will struggled over wanting to quit. *Just put one foot in front of the other,* I kept telling myself. Each quarter mile threatened to be my last. The breathing came in shorter pants, my lungs burned. My legs refused to cooperate. I thought how crazy I was out there on the road, a grown man jogging up a hill. But I kept on anyway. Only my sheer determination to complete the ten-mile goal kept me charging forward.

I can always walk, I reminded myself. I also knew that once I reached the end of the fifth mile, I would be at the halfway point. From then on, it was returning the same way I had come. That fifth mile seemed to stretch out forever.

I made the turn at Garden Walk Boulevard, breathed deeply, and even though my pace had slowed, started the sixth mile. Something happened to me within the next half mile. Some call it a second wind or a runner's high. Maybe I had just come alive. All I know is that the weary bones no longer rebelled. My breathing sounded normal. There was less pain in my lungs. My legs picked up the pace.

My strides were longer, and I felt a rhythm and a grace in my movement. The last two miles were sheer joy, and I sprinted the last two-tenths of a mile at top speed.

Reflecting on the experience reminds me that life works that way sometimes. We start out the day slow, depressed, downhearted, sure we can't make it. We wail, "Lord, help me."

When we cry out for help, we're not even sure if God will come to our aid. We pray simply because we don't know what else to do. Yet, even those emergency prayers which act like arrows we shoot upward get heard. That's when we realize the truth of verses such as, "He gives power to the faint, and to him who has no might he increases strength."

Whether we talk of running or our jobs or coping with mental pressures, God's promise still stands before us—he gives power to those ready to give up.

He gives strength to the weary.

Almighty Father, remind me that with your help I can complete every task because I have your strength. Amen.

COMPULSION

Let your moderation be known unto all . . .(Philippians 4:5 KJV)

Week 3, Day 2

Gene runs, a lot, seemingly every day. Some weeks he streaks down the roads and streets and chalks up over a hundred miles. Sound impressive? Depends on who you talk to.

Ask Gene's wife and children how they react. Marcia says, "Tuesday he came home from work at 5:07, lay down for a brief nap. Half an hour later, he dashed down the steps, wearing running gear." She moaned, "Dinner will be ready in ten minutes." He only waved as he tore off down the street. Gene returned at 9:30, after his daughters were in bed.

Each year Gene signs up for two or three marathons. He's now preparing for an ultra-marathon of fifty miles. Yet six years ago Gene hadn't even tied on his first pair of Nike shoes. Then a friend interested him in the sport. Within two years he ran in 10K (6.3 miles) races, winning two of them for his age division.

Those victories spurred Gene on. Since then, he's constantly figuring out how to increase his speed or prolong his endurance. He buys the latest lightweight shoes and reads all the literature. Those of us who know him admit that Gene is probably the best runner around. If he had started earlier, some think he might even be of world-class caliber.

However, in his striving to run better, Gene has forgotten something. The Bible calls it moderation, the opposite of compulsiveness. Moderation urges balance, a time for all important things in our lives, rather than being obsessed by one idea or activity. Even when Gene is not running, he admits it's the most frequent thing on his mind.

In a sense, Gene is like the compulsive drinker or gambler. He's miserable except when he runs. He's always figuring out ways to get out of activities and obligations in order to spend more time with the sport which has become his master.

After having run a few years, I understand Gene's situation. It happens to many who get serious about running. It almost caught me.

I reached the level of a consistent thirty miles a week. That didn't satisfy a drive within me. I kept trying to figure how I could juggle my schedule so I could run forty miles every week. For two months in the summer of 1980 I averaged over forty miles a week. That meant I had to run at least five days a week instead of four.

One day I ran thirteen miles and came home too tired to do anything but elevate my feet in front of the television and fall asleep. The next night, after only eight miles, I fell asleep again. The following morning I asked myself, "Why do I need to run forty miles a week?"

For several days I prayed about my compulsive need to add miles. Forty miles a week demanded more time and energy, which I needed to devote to other activities. And where would the cycle end?—more miles and faster speeds. The inner compulsion would not stop.

Immediately I cut back to thirty miles a week. One week I had completed only twenty-three miles by Friday and knew I could make up the seven on Saturday. However, I was a little tired so I decided not to run that day. I had broken the compulsion. Now I could enjoy running with moderation again.

For the next three weeks after making my decision to cut down on my mileage, I actually had to pray, "Lord, help me *not* run so many miles this week."

I also asked, "Let running be fun and not my master. I need one Master."

My Master and my God, give me only one compulsion in life—following you. Amen.

WHEN EVERYTHING GOES WRONG

You will keep in perfect peace all who trust in you, all whose thoughts are fixed on you! (Isaiah 26:3)

Week 3, Day 3

By noon Tuesday I couldn't even smile. There were bags under my eyes. I stooped slightly and felt 400 years old. The glue had disappeared in everyone's relationships. Phone calls the day before, with late-evening counseling, were followed by more phone calls Tuesday. That morning I learned of discipline problems in the Sunday school which exceeded the ability of the department head. Two teachers wouldn't speak to each other and asked me to moderate. A much-loved man in the church died suddenly of a heart attack. A friend called at 11:30 A.M., telling me on the phone that her boss had fired her. She cried, asking again and again, "What am I going to do?"

By noon, when I had completed the call, I had to get away from the office. I felt like going home to bed and sleeping for thirty hours with the phone off the hook and the doorbell disconnected.

Tuesday is also one of my running days. "Oh, Lord, I don't feel like running now," I said as I got into my car. Ordinarily I would have made it a ten-mile run, but I couldn't get excited about jogging ten feet.

Fortunately the habit had been firmly established within me to run even when my mind said, *Ah, don't bother today.* I argued with myself and threw up a few quick questions to the Lord for guidance. Finally I said, "I'll just make it a short one today. Enough to loosen up a bit, work up a sweat and then I'll stop."

That "short one" stretched to eight miles. When I returned to the office, my secretary glanced up. A surprised smile creased her face and she chirped, "You look fifty percent better than when you left."

I felt much better, too. The run had enabled me to push all those pressures away. I thought of the man who had died, my friend who had lost her job. But they no longer weighed me down. The problems had not shrunk, but I could now cope with all of them.

Part of the change occurred because I pray as I run. I talk to the Lord about the problems and pressures. I enjoy the scenery, wave at people, think of the temperature, wonder about the weather, even think about my running form.

Somewhere during the run my mind moves into another gear. Those concerns lose their intensity and urgency. Sometimes I daydream. Other times I plan an activity with my wife or with a friend.

Some days I'm struggling with an article. It just isn't going right. Often during the entire run I don't even consciously think about it. Yet when I come back to my office and can squeeze time out to write again, suddenly it has worked out for me and I know what to say next.

Many of the ways of the mind we can't explain. I do know this: that after starting to jog with a stress-filled body, I finish up with what the Apostle Paul assures us, "His peace will guard your hearts and minds as you live in Christ Jesus" (Philippians 4:7). Then you will experience God's peace, which exceeds anything we can understand.

No matter how wrong everything else may be today, keep everything right between you and me as you fill me with your perfect peace. Amen.

BEATING ANXIETY

*"That is why I tell you not to worry about everyday life—
whether you have enough food and drink, or enough clothes
to wear. Isn't life more than food, and your body more than
clothing?" (Matthew 6:25)*

Week 3, Day 4

No one needs to tell us about stress and tension in
our society. It's there, in all of us. We also know
that running is one helpful cure for the problem.

God equipped our bodies to handle stress. Our
muscles tense for action and then don't do anything.
Repeated tensing of those muscles results in physio-
logical problems ranging from spasm and back pain
to tearing of muscles.

An important principle is that stress on one system relaxes another. When one part of us, such as
our intellect, reaches the high-tension level, we do
better to change to a physical activity.

Running is one of the ways to beat stress.
Someone has said, "It's impossible to jog and worry
at the same time."

William Glasser, in his book *Positive Addiction,* states that he believes a person who jogs one mile a day increases in self-confidence and imaginative powers. These two things work against stress and anxiety.

Just today I put antianxiety tactics to work. As a volunteer chaplain I spent most of the morning at the local hospital. I talked to twenty-six patients. I stayed with a few of them as long as ten minutes, hearing their sad experiences and praying for them. One twenty-year-old man cried as he faced surgery. Another patient expressed fears of never getting well again.

When I left the hospital, I felt emotionally drained, tense, and then thought of all the things I needed to do at the church. My first impulse was to grab a quick lunch and spend the afternoon working away at the stacks of papers on my desk. Instead, I went home, changed, and ran for an hour. Then I went to the office with a new energy level, and I completed what appeared to be three days' work in less than three hours.

It is now 5:15, and I'm going to leave the office in a few minutes. The running may have interrupted my day, but it also eased my tension and erased my anxieties.

While recognizing that running may not be for everybody and it's not the cure for everything, it's still one of the best cures for anxiety (and cheap, too!). No matter how heavy my load—mental or emotional—when I finish running I have beat the anxiety pains. Those problems which threatened to overwhelm me don't seem important anymore.

Jesus said, ". . . I tell you not to worry about everyday life—whether you have enough food and drink, or enough clothes to wear. Isn't life more than food, and your body more than clothing?" (Matthew 6:25) In that verse and the verses following, Jesus exhorted us not to be anxious because God is with us. Nothing happens to us outside of the Lord's loving care. But sometimes we're so anxiety laden we can't hear those words.

Running is one of the ways to clear away the anxiety so that we can read and appreciate Jesus' words.

Mighty God, release me from anxiety and remind me of your continual care. Amen.

OVERCOMING BOREDOM

Finally, brethren, whatever is true, whatever is honorable, whatever is just, whatever is pure, whatever is lovely, whatever is gracious, if there is any excellence, if there is anything worthy of praise, think about these things. What you have learned and received and heard and seen in me, do; and the God of peace will be with you. (Philippians 4:8, 9)

Week 3, Day 5

A sports commentator on TV evaluated individual sports such as cycling and swimming. His final comment about running went like this: "For all the good things you can say about running, I never could stick with it. I found it boring."

Apparently he expressed a prevalent attitude. And some people do find running a boring sport. But it really depends on what you do with your mind while you run.

The would-be runners who concentrate on how far they've come and how far they have to go, who think only of their discomfort and peek at their watches every thirty-three seconds, get bored.

I have a few ideas about what to do with our minds when we run. These ideas have come to me as I've jogged on tracks, streets, and roads. I've made my time not only good physical exercise, but mentally profitable as well.

For a full year I memorized Scripture. I typed verses on little cards that fitted easily into the palm of my hand. I found that I could memorize approximately one verse a mile. (However, after memorizing three hundred verses and reviewing them, the reviewing process became hard to keep up with. Eventually I stopped memorizing.)

Another helpful idea: Carry a prayer list. I often do this. By holding the list in my hand and glancing at it from time to time, my mind focuses on spiritual things. As the apostle writes, "Whatever is true… honorable…just…pure…lovely…gracious…think about these things."

Jogging often becomes problem-solving time for me. I'm stuck on a situation demanding a decision. In my head I play out all the possibilities. I ask the Lord's counsel. Decisions don't usually come then, but the problem has been laid out. Later, when I get back to the problem, I often find the solution absolutely obvious. But I know the grappling for an answer went on while I trekked down the street.

Occasionally my mind floats free, as it did this past Saturday. The trees had just clothed themselves in green. Jonquils flowered by the side of several driveways. Shrubs showed the buds which would soon burst open. Appreciation and praise for the beauty of this world flowed from me. I thanked God for his creation and color, for the warm sunshine. I remember also giving thanks for the special people in my life. As I did an eight-mile run, I thought "About these things."

God, teach me to enjoy life—every part of it—and keep my mind filled with you as I go through today's activities. Amen.

DEPRESSION

Why am I discouraged? Why is my heart so sad? I will put my hope in God! I will praise him again—my Savior and my God! (Psalm 42:5)

Week 3, Day 6

Depression hit me hard. I couldn't throw it off all morning. *Marie's dead,* I kept thinking. She had been so alive the day before, smiling, making plans. She underwent coronary-artery bypass surgery, and the doctor had expected recovery. But because of other medical problems, she died seventeen hours after surgery.

Marie had been active in our church, helping us form a Sunday-school class for divorced singles. She had encouraged and strengthened many when they felt cast down and discouraged.

I dragged through until midafternoon. Things I needed to do no longer seemed important. I couldn't rise above the grief and sense of loss. Finally I went for a five-mile run in the rain. I came back, still sad, but my depression had lifted. I felt normal again.

For me, running has proved valuable in coping with depression. There was a time when I could mope around and ask, as the psalmist did, "Why are you cast down, O my soul?" Now I run.

Something about vigorous activity dulls the impact of negative feelings. Running roots out anger, lessens anxiety, and breaks down hostility.

I see depressed people all the time. They visit my office; they call me on the phone. They're sluggish. They do a minimum of physical movement.

I've often thought that if I had to characterize depressed people by a physical position, I would use words such as *sitting* or *lying down*. That was the position of Elijah when he went through a tough time (1 Kings 19:4) "I have had enough, LORD," he said. "Take my life, for I am no better than my ancestors who have already died" (1 Kings 19:4).

In low times people want to shut themselves away from others. They take the phone off the hook, crawl under the covers, and sleep. Or they sit and stare at nothing for hours. The more they think, the more they brood and fill their minds with morbid thoughts.

Yet when those same people get their marvelously made bodies into action, things change. They may experience physical tiredness, but they also feel better about life and about themselves.

In the years I've been jogging, I've never felt depressed at the end of a workout. I've had aching legs, blistered heels and toes, once or twice even muscle cramps, but never depression. I groan and strain during the run. But when it's all over and I stand under the shower, I find myself singing and enjoying life. I always like myself a lot more and believe God is pleased that I'm trying to take good care of his holy temple.

Thanks, Lord Jesus, for lifting my spirits. With your help, I can overcome all my obstacles. Amen.

SHELF LIFE

"I am leaving you with a gift—peace of mind and heart. And the peace I give is a gift the world cannot give. So don't be troubled or afraid." (John 14:27)

Week 3, Day 7

"You're not a real runner until you've had at least one injury," the expert said in a lecture. He told us about the common injuries—shin splints, stress fractures, blisters, and runner's knee.

"Odd," he said, "running improves our hearts and lungs and protects us from stroke, heart attack, and other diseases, but it also brings its own special medical problems. Most commonly they show up as blisters and sore feet, but they can also be serious. Some runners have to sit out the sport for weeks at a time."

I'm one of the fortunate ones. In five years of running I've never had any injury, but I've talked to those who have had to give up the sport for a while.

A friend reminds me of a statement I heard by someone else long ago. Mel underwent surgery and a long recuperative period. He said, "I guess God has put me on the shelf."

That happens to most of us at some time in life. When we're sick is the most noticeable time. We may not like it, but we may need to be put on the shelf temporarily. We overtrain our bodies. We undergo extreme pressures. We skip needed sleep.

In our lives, as in the lives of people with any real sickness, illness may be God's method of putting us on a shelf-temporarily.

Then one day he who put us there, takes us down. We find we've recharged our spiritual batteries. We've restocked our priorities in life and have begun putting first things first again. We return to circulation—running, walking, back into the mainstream.

We need to remind ourselves, however, that even when we're on the shelf, we're not alone. God doesn't forget us. Even in those times when we're restricted, laid up, or unable to participate fully in life, God has not forgotten us. Knowing that the shelving is only temporary gives us peace—the genuine peace that comes only from God.

Lord, whether I'm on the shelf today or running at my best, you are with me. Your peace is mine always. Remind me of that throughout the day. Amen.

Hard Progress

Peter declared, "Even if everyone else deserts you, I will never desert you." (Matthew 26:33)

Week 4, Day 1

Most people know all the stories of Peter. He's the apostle who often spoke first and thought later—as he chewed on the foot lodged firmly in his mouth. One of those statements had to do with the betrayal of Jesus.

As part of God's plan for our salvation, Jesus had to die, an innocent man for the guilty. When the Lord told his first followers of his death, they didn't understand. They did not understand either the plan or themselves.

Then Peter did it again. He spoke before he knew what he was doing. "Not me, Jesus. I'll never betray you." But, of course, he did. Three times he denied even knowing the Lord.

I have a lot of sympathy for Peter. In his zeal he often overestimated his abilities, or perhaps underestimated the difficulties.

A lot of us do that. We make commitments with our heads that our bodies can't keep. In running,

I've sometimes decided I would run a dozen miles that day. Why not? I felt energetic and had the time. But either because I put too much energy into the first miles or because I underestimated the fatigue from twelve miles, I quit early.

We, to, overestimate our abilities and underestimate the demands of our task. Unfortunately, that's how most of us learn. We make mistakes, poor judgments, inaccurate calculations. Newborn Christians want to mature quickly and often get overinvolved in church activities. They pledge more than they can actually afford to give.

I've reminded myself of that lesson when I want to progress in my running. The temptation for newcomers to the sport is to increase speed and mileage too quickly. They do one mile without much effort, and the next week they want to increase to five.

Fortunately I resisted that urge. As I got comfortable with two miles, I moved up to two and a half and did not increase that for at least three weeks. Then I added another half mile. I took longer to run six miles than two of my friends who spurted from two to six almost immediately. However, I'm still running. One of them incurred constant shin splints and stopped. The other dropped out and now plays tennis instead.

In learning about myself through running, through day-to-day activities, and through my spiritual experiences, I can better estimate my abilities. I learn also to accept my limitations.

Our Father, thank you for the abilities I have. Thank you for my limitations. Help me perceive both. Amen.

WEIGHTED RUNNING

Therefore, since we are surrounded by such a huge crowd of witnesses to the life of faith, let us strip off every weight that slows us down, especially the sin that so easily trips us up. And let us run with endurance the race God has set before us. (Hebrews 12:1)

Week 4, Day 2

A Greek myth tells about Atalanta, a huntress nursed from infancy by a bear. As she grew older, she gained fame for her physical prowess, by hunting and running faster than any man. When Atalanta reached marriageable age, she turned down her suitors. "I will only marry the man who can outrun me," she said.

The challengers came. Atalanta defeated and humiliated them all. Her father had all the would-be husbands killed.

One bright fellow named Hippomenes (in some books they call him Milanion) came along. He knew that he could not possibly outrun her. He had to figure out a way to beat her, become her husband, and inherit half of the vast kingdom. After weeks of thought, Hippomenes came up with a sure-fire way to win.

The two started the race, and Hippomenes gave a great burst of speed which he knew he could not maintain. As soon as Atalanta got close to him, he pulled a golden apple out of a bag he carried, dropped it, and moved on. She, knowing she could pass the man easily, stopped, and picked up the golden object.

Minutes later she was ready to pass him again, and Hippomenes dropped another golden apple. She picked it up. The farther they ran, the heavier Atalanta's load became. By the time he had rid himself of his load and she had picked up every apple, he easily won the race, and the hand of Atalanta.

I always think of that mythical race when I read Hebrews 12. The exhortation to "lay aside every weight" makes that story flash into my mind. One runner dropped his burden, the other only accumulated more weight. Over the course of several miles, Hippomenes easily won. He had stripped himself of everything that held him back. Atalanta merely weighted herself down.

We know that in running, the more weight we carry, the harder the race. The fleetest runners wear the lightest shoes and clothes. They're also trim, with almost no body fat. They want nothing impeding them.

As we run the race of life, we're not always so concerned with burdens we carry. Many find themselves loaded down with debts, worries sometimes.

Guilt puts more weight on us than most of us acknowledge.

Perhaps the writer of Hebrews understood this, for he says not only to lay aside weights but also "sin which clings so closely." He exhorts us to have nothing holding us back in our race to follow Jesus Christ. And every weight must ultimately have one name: sin.

No matter what the weight, or how insignificant it may seem, if we allow it to burden us, it impedes our growth and it is sin. These clinging weights come upon us easily.

Even so, we can lay them aside. Through the help of God's Spirit, we can cast aside every weight and "run with perseverance the race that is set before us."

God, I surrender my burdens to you today because you're the world's best weight lifter. Amen.

Mind Setting

Fix your thoughts on what is true, and honorable, and right, and pure, and lovely, and admirable. Think about things that are excellent and worthy of praise. Keep putting into practice all you learned and received from me—everything you heard from me and saw me doing. Then the God of peace will be with you. (Philippians 4:8–9)

Week 4, Day 3

Writing the book had started well. After seeing an outline and three chapters, the publisher gave me a contract. I whizzed away page after page. I had completed more than half the book when my creative flow stopped. I read the outline several times and nothing happened. Determined, I sat at my typewriter, made several stabs at a paragraph and finally, in disgust, wadded up the paper.

Not expecting any improvement in the situation, I went for a ten-mile run. I purposely did not think about the book. Instead, I wanted to clear my mind and enjoy a period of quietness. I ran along a seldom-used, winding road, lined with hardwood trees on both sides. It was late spring and unusually warm. Chipmunks scampered down trees, and starlings flew overhead. I especially noticed a small lake I could see from the top of the hill.

Part of the time I talked with God. Mostly I watched the action of his creatures and appreciated his world. Although few words passed from my mouth, I experienced communion with the Lord.

I needed that time away from my typewriter. That eighty minutes of running was a period of meditation for me. Running meditation means turning my thoughts to him, and yet allowing them to float freely. Sometimes I silently hold up a problem. Other times names and faces of friends come before me, and I pray for them. Mostly I enjoy being alive and being with God.

When I come back to my desk after having left with a clogged brain, I'm suddenly more alert. The writing flows. On that particular day (my last day of vacation) I had determined to have at least 160 pages completed. I sat down, scarcely looked at my outline, and the ideas filled my head. My fingers could hardly keep up with my mind as they pecked across the keyboard. I finished the draft of that chapter in less than an hour.

I've shared this experience with others, and they call it everything from prayer to creative brooding. It doesn't matter what we call it. *Meditation* is good enough for me. I fill my mind with thoughts of the pure, the lovely, the good. When running, my creative powers seem to expand and open themselves wide. And why not? I'm in contact with the God who created this wonderful universe. He also created me. I have set my mind on him, and he fills my mind with the ideas to put on paper.

Father, help me set my mind on you today. Fill me with a sense of your presence. Amen.

New Every Time

The faithful love of the LORD never ends! His mercies never cease. Great is his faithfulness; his mercies begin afresh each morning. (Lamentations 3:22, 23)

Week 4, Day 4

Something had happened in my running. I had sensed it for over a week. It involved getting started. My bones felt old, and each step was torturous. Not painful, but cumbersome, like an old man. Once I had finished three or four miles, that all disappeared. But time after time it came in that first mile.

I tried to explain this to my wife, using an analogy of the Plymouth we owned back in the days before automatic transmissions. For some reason our battery frequently went dead, even a new battery. We learned to park on the top of hills and we'd put the car in neutral, push the vehicle until it picked up a little speed, then hop in, turn the key, and the car started immediately. From then on, we had a smooth ride. That's how I felt about running—it took me a mile before I turned on the key

I've thought of two reasons for this. First, the body needs a little time to move from first gear into overdrive. But second, as I become more sensitive to my "body speech" I realize that I'm taking this human machine from a sedentary position and throwing it into full gear. It takes as least a mile for my body to make the adjustment.

And I go through this each time I run. Now that I understand, it doesn't disturb me.

As I've thought about starting new every day, it helps me make a parallel with the Bible. Lamentations tells us about God's mercies—they never cease. "They are new every morning."

Some nights I lie in bed, reviewing my activities of the day. My failures rush to my thoughts, words I didn't say but ought to have, or rash statements which would have been better if left unsaid. Then I remind myself, *God forgives me.* I know that my failures are wiped away. Then I can sleep.

When I awaken in the morning and greet the new day, it is like entering into a fresh, new world. I have the opportunity to start all over again. Sometimes it's awkward, but it's also wonderful. I experience the mercies of God through the day as I float across a footpath, through the closeness of my wife as we hold hands at the breakfast table, through the loving encouragement of friends who love me and take time to express it.

In those moments I can't do better than repeat the words of the prophet: "The steadfast love of the Lord never ceases, his mercies never come to an end; they are new every morning...." I also find myself ending with the next line he uses, "...Great is thy faithfulness."

Creator God, thank you for today. Make me aware of the newness of each day as another example of your love. Amen.

BETTER LOVERS

"So now I am giving you a new commandment: Love each other. Just as I have loved you, you should love each other. Your love for one another will prove to the world that you are my disciples." (John 13:34–35)

Week 4, Day 5

RUNNERS MAKE BETTER LOVERS, the bumper sticker read. I smiled as I jogged past the parked car. I'd heard fleet-footed men boast of that before. There may even be truth in the assertion.

They claim that with leaner bodies, runners have a greater sense of self-confidence, which enhances their total well-being. This also stimulates their sexual responses. A healthy body promotes healthy attitudes. And, they add, runners not only feel better, but they have a stronger libido.

Whether these statements bear true or not, they do make me think of love. Not so much sexual love as the frequent New Testament word *love* (Greek: *agape*)—not merely an emotional experience, but a principle of the mind and will. It is an attitude and an achievement, an attitude of mind, an action that works toward good for all people, no matter who they are.

When I think of love in that sense, I recall the words of Jesus. One of the last things he said to his disciples on the night of his betrayal was, "By this all men will know that you are my disciples, if you have love for one another."

As I race through the Atlanta suburb where I live, I often reflect on the statements of Jesus, especially this one. I think not so much on the quantity of my love, but on my lack.

For instance, the other day, a conviction ripped at my guts—I had stored up anger against someone else. As the awareness hit me, I prayed for God to help me love and forgive this man. He had made untrue accusations and even hurled out a few insults. The real issue for me was not his guilt or failure, but my lack of love. I found it hard to forgive. I kept thinking, *He owes me an apology at least.* I couldn't seem to let go of my stirred-up anger.

Jogging up a steep incline, my pace slowed and I puffed harder. When I finally reached the place where the road leveled off, I said to myself, *I finally made it to the top.*

That moment made me realize that loving some people is like trudging up a hill. It's hard work. I want to quit. I perspire and find all kinds of excuses for turning around. But I don't quit because that's where I have to go. I keep on moving, placing one foot in front of the other.

In a way I can't explain, in that moment I forgave the other person. I had struggled and it had not been easy, but I had won. He has not apologized, and he may never acknowledge his mistakes. That no longer matters.

Jesus said, "Your love for one another will prove to the world that you are my disciples" (John 13:35).

Loving Lord Jesus, make me a better lover. Amen.

RUN FUN

*Work hard so you can present yourself to God and receive
his approval. Be a good worker, one who does not need to
be ashamed and who correctly explains the word of truth.
(2 Timothy 2:15)*

Week 4, Day 6

The Swedes have a word for it. They call it *fartlek,*
which means "speed play." This word rolled into
the runner's vocabulary because of the work of Gosta
Holmer, chief coach of the Swedish team in the 1948
Olympics. Essentially, *fartlek* refers to a free-style running over an indefinite distance for an indefinite time.

Fartlek consists of fast, untimed runs over various
distances and different terrains, often in groups.
The runners alternate between fast and slow, and
allow each individual to change speeds. The goal is
to make the workout *fun.*

The idea centers on frequent change of pace.
For instance, they charge the hills and slow down on
the downward slope. They glide along for a mile at
a medium pace, then accelerate, slow down, sprint,
even run backwards for fifty yards.

Long before running, I discovered the principle of *fartlek* in my devotional time. After being a Christian fifteen years, I began having problems. While I firmly believed in reading the Bible and praying each day, I also had to fight boredom, especially in reading.

While acknowledging it's a divine Book, the daily routine of reading the same book over and over opens one to monotony. The most helpful thing I've done for myself is to vary my reading. Shifting to another translation sometimes adds new insight to a verse. Instead of reading books straight through, I've used commentaries as guides. I keep looking for variations to keep the Bible fresh.

The same with prayer. For a while I use a prayer list, then abandon it and pray largely for people and needs as I remember them. One day I'll go for a long walk and pray audibly as I trek through my neighborhood. Other times I'm on my knees beside my bed. One day I fill my prayer time with nothing but praise and thanksgiving. I've had a few occasions where I've been burdened with a problem or a sense of failure and spent the entire time in repentance and self-searching.

Like the *fartlek* of running, I search for ways to avoid monotony in the Christian life. I want to keep encountering Jesus Christ in fresh and exciting ways.

Father God, let me meet you today in a fresh way. Help me enjoy being a Christian. Amen.

HITTING THE WALL

But those who trust in the Lord will find new strength. They will soar high on wings like eagles. They will run and not grow weary. They will walk and not faint. (Isaiah 40:31)

Week 4, Day 7

Marathoners often talk about "hitting the wall." For most of them, especially the ones new to the grueling demands of 26.2 miles, they know it too well. They run along, depleting their energy and strength, but still moving. Then they awaken to the fact that they can't make it anymore. They've exhausted themselves.

Hitting the wall—the nemesis of runners. We know the experience outside the jogging track as well. You wake up one morning forty-five years old and realize you're in a dead-end job. You're gone as far as you can go. That's the wall.

You've been married for twelve years, and you admit the two of you no longer have a vital, living relationship. You are merely two people who share the same house.

You've tried to teach your children to follow Christ, and now they live in rebellion. You've tried everything to reach them, but their ears become like walls which close you out.

In these and dozens of other situations, what do we do?

We have at least three options: *We can fight.* This attitude says, "I'm gritting my teeth, and I'm going to make it even if I have to crawl. I'm going through that wall."

We stop and give up. We're convinced that the situation is hopeless, and we can't find a solution. We've passed the point of endurance. It's not worth fighting anymore.

We accept it. By accepting, we adjust to life the way it is now. We have no power to change; so we adapt to our new world.

Many hard-rock situations present us with a dilemma. We have no easy answers for many everyday problems. However, we do have the promise in Isaiah 40:31. When we wait upon the Lord (when we pray and wait for his direction), he gives us the answer by renewing our strength. We can then hold out a little longer. We can adapt with grace. We can surrender with strength and peace.

The wall may not be the end at all. Instead it can be an opportunity, an opportunity for us to show God that we need him, an opportunity for God to respond to us. It's a confession of our weakness and our need for his strength. Hitting the wall says,

"Okay, Lord, here's where I need you to take over. I'll never make it without your help."

Then God comes through. We who felt we couldn't make it one more step find ourselves soaring like the eagle.

My teacher and my God, help me learn once and for all that when problems overwhelm me, that's your opportunity to take over and deliver me. Amen.

FOLLOWING

[Paul said,] So I urge you to imitate me. (1 Corinthians 4:16)

"Follow me and be my disciple," Jesus said to him. So Levi got up and followed him. (Mark 2:14)

Week 5, Day 1

Sometimes I think of the words of the Apostle Paul in 1 Corinthians 4:16, urging us to follow. Most modern translators use the word *imitator* which is really closer to the original language. It's as though the apostle has found his stride; he's leading the pack and may even be quite a distance ahead. Can you visualize his turning his head, motioning with his arm, and yelling, "Follow me!?"

Or when we visualize the stories of Jesus calling his original disciples, we think of Peter and James and John at their nets and Jesus walking by. Or Jesus strolling up to Levi the tax collector. That may be the actual case. But in my mind I like to use a different picture. I like to think of Jesus whizzing by, racing toward Calvary. And when he approaches Levi, he calls out, "Follow me." And Levi dumps his record books and money bag and joins the race.

Shifting into that mind-set brings meaning to my concept of life. I think of running as more than motion. It's a way of thinking about life.

For us, although we don't run to achieve a spiritual experience or the runner's high, every run can be a spiritual experience for us. We can think of each trek as following after Christ.

Sometimes I think of myself finishing up the course of life, and I think of the words of Paul to Timothy: "...have finished the race, and I have remained faithful. And now the prize awaits me—the crown of righteousness" (2 Timothy 4:7, 8).

The next time you run, and you find your energy fleeing, why not think of the exhortation of Paul: "imitate me," or the simple command of Jesus: "Follow me." Think of the excitement of running through life, your eyes riveted on Jesus who leads the way.

I'm following you, Lord Jesus. Don't let me lag behind. Amen.

Are You Running
With Me, Jesus?

"Teach these new disciples to obey all the commands I have given you. And be sure of this: I am with you always, even to the end of the age." (Matthew 28:20)

Week 5, Day 2

In the 1960s Malcom Boyd wrote a book with the fascinating title *Are You Running With Me, Jesus?* He offered a penetrating look at attitudes for that period of "flower power."

That's a good question for all of us to ask ourselves regularly. *Are you keeping up with me, Lord, as I gallop through life? Are you running with me, Jesus, as I progress in my profession? in my marriage on in my singleness?*

We ask because we need assurance that we made the right decisions. Or we're regretting our choices. We make right and left turns in life based on what we believe at the time is best for us. Many of us pray for guidance. We rush into new ventures, convinced that we're entering the happiest period of our lives.

Then the glory of the decision wears off. The new house has construction flaws. Marriage isn't all we dreamed it would be. Living the single life isn't quite as exciting as we had expected. Our new jobs pay more money, but the stress increases. That's when we pause and ask, "Are you running with me, Jesus?"

The answer is *yes*. Without qualification.

That doesn't mean he approves of all our choices. It may mean that Jesus is trying to get us to change directions. He lets our dream world cave in, but he's not fighting us.

Even when I'm wandering from the right path, God's still at my side. He's there to talk to and to listen to. I've learned that when I make a wrong turn or run in the wrong direction, the Lord has been beside me whispering. I haven't always heard. Sometimes I've been too intense in the race itself; other times too concerned about what I wanted. Even when I've ignored his presence, he still keeps up with me.

In those moments when it appears as though I'm alone, I think of his promises, especially Matthew 28:20. The statement contains the last recorded words of Jesus in Matthew's Gospel. He gave the command for them to teach, preach, and disciple. But even more important, he added, "...lo, I am with you always...."

You're always running with me, Jesus. Make me aware of your presence today. Amen.

CAMARADERIE

Two people are better off than one, for they can help each other succeed. If one person falls, the other can reach out and help. But someone who falls alone is in real trouble. Likewise, two people lying close together can keep each other warm. But how can one be warm alone? A person standing alone can be attacked and defeated, but two can stand back-to-back and conquer. Three are even better, for a triple-braided cord is not easily broken. (Ecclesiastes 4: 9–12)

Week 5, Day 3

Howard invited me to go to the health spa with him, and in a sense he introduced me to the whole realm of physical fitness. When it came to running, Shirley and I made the decision to start it together. Peter urged me to join him in a 3.1 race, or I might never have gotten started racing.

Perhaps because we're basically social beings, few of us like to start new ventures alone. This also may have something to say about the concept of marriage. The Apostle Paul speaks (in quoting Genesis) about husband and wife becoming one. They become one, but they're still two people.

And one of the best things a friend or a mate can do is to encourage. When one is down, the other encourages. When one is ill, the other serves.

Certainly in running—at least in the beginning—it takes a second person for most of us to get started. I needed Shirley's encouragement.

I thought about running. But I also thought of this middle-aged man, with bulging stomach and awkward form, stumbling along for the whole world to see. I felt self-conscious that first morning. But with Shirley by my side, certainly no thinner than I—and she didn't run like a graceful gazelle—I persevered.

Even though I no longer need the presence of another, having another alongside still makes the running more pleasant. And for me, this is nowhere more evident than in 5K and 10K races.

In one of our first 10K runs, my daughter and I trudged along Stone Mountain in Georgia. The hill seemed never to end. We looked at each other and smiled, too tired to make conversation. Just then two teenage girls caught up with us.

"Hey, want us to pull you to the top?" one of them called.

"No, just let me hold onto you," I said and laughed.

Two miles later we saw those sprinters out of juice. They had stopped running and walked up the hill.

"Hey, need a push?" I called out.

"A complete overhaul's what I want," one of them said and waved.

That's the spirit of camaraderie that's special in the running game. Most of us enjoy the sport, don't take it too seriously, and appreciate the fellowship with other runners.

It's much like the church to me. Christians who have the commonality of Jesus Christ in their lives have that same sort of camaraderie. They share a common love for Jesus Christ. By their commitment to Christ, they also commit themselves to strengthening each other.

Lord God, thanks for my Christian brothers and sisters. We share a special fellowship because of our relationship with you. Amen.

THE PERFECT RUNNER

But you are to be perfect, even as your Father in heaven is perfect. (Matthew 5:28)

Week 5, Day 4

After less than a year of running, euphoric dreams filled my head. I could see trophies, medals, and awards covering the walls of my den. Why not? I had increased my weekly mileage from zero to twelve and often fourteen miles My time had gone from an embarrassing thirteen minutes a mile (half of it walking) to a so-so eight minutes. If I could improve that much in a year....

I pictured myself in tee shirt and shorts, winning local 10K races, and then moving on to mini-marathons and eventually entering marathons. The running bug had bitten. The fever spread all through my system. Running eased itself into one of my primary topics of conversation. Let someone mention the subject and I sounded like the zealous devotee of a new cult.

This running craze didn't lie only in the realm of dreams. I set goals for myself. By the end of the next six months, I would average seven and a half minutes a mile, then move on to seven. Eventually I hoped to reach of goal of five minutes a mile. Why shouldn't I make it?

In the middle of my second year of running, a sad truth sank in: I would never rise to the level of championship running. If I had started running by my early twenties, it might have been possible. If I had committed more time and greater amounts of energy to the sport, with more intensive workouts, I might have reached some of those goals. But one day I admitted to myself, *Cec, you're not going to fulfill that dream of a 26.2 marathon, averaging five minutes a mile.* More than that, I wouldn't even win a 10K.

As I grow older, a stark truth confronts me: I'll never fulfill all my ambitions. In my teens and twenties, I believed I could do anything I set for a goal. My dreams exceeded my ability, but in the back of my head I always thought I could still do it if I chose. If not today, one day.

Now I know I'll never be a perfect runner, nor a perfect husband, certainly not a perfect Christian.

Realizing that fact brought me into a perplexity recently when I read again the Sermon on the Mount. Jesus said, "Be perfect."

Perfection isn't possible in any real of life. So what do I do? Give up? Certainly not!

I think of life much like the song that speaks about reaching for the unreachable star or beating unbeatable foes. I don't give up simply because I don't attain. The joy isn't in achieving, anyway. The joy comes through the struggle.

As a Christian and as a runner, I'm stretching all the time. I'm trying to get better. In running, praying, preaching—in all areas—someone is always better or faster or smarter, but it doesn't deter me. I'm still aiming for perfection.

Heavenly Father, even though I'll never be perfect, keep me trying. Amen.

ALONE WITH MYSELF

One evening as [Isaac] was walking and meditating in the fields, he looked up and saw the camels coming. (Genesis 24:63)

Week 5, Day 5

Shirley and I went on a ten-day tour of Israel with 150 other Christians. I learned much about the land of the Bible. I also learned something about myself during those days: my need for privacy.

Every day we jumped into buses immediately after breakfast. We toured together all day, ate our meals together, talked, sang, and prayed together— all lovely people with no disagreeable types ruining the trip. Yet by the fifth day I had to get away from the crowd. I had gone on short runs two mornings after breakfast and before the buses arrived. But that wasn't enough.

I like people. I like being around them. I'm in the people-serving business. It shocked me to discover that I needed to separate myself from the crowd. Restlessness and a sense of being hemmed in made me yearn for open spaces without other people.

Since that trip, I've been more aware of the way I function. When I've seen several people in one day, all with heavy problems, I need to back away. Take today, for instance. First a woman came by who needed food and help in paying her rent. I spent time on the phone calling various agencies. Later, another woman with severe marital problems and a rebellious teenage daughter talked to me for almost an hour. Still later, a young man, facing his future, not sure which way to go, came in. His father pushes him one way, and he wants to go another direction. Then just before lunch Rachel called. Her mother has been told she has a terminal illness. She cried on the phone for at least half an hour. Then I had lunch with an attractive twenty-year-old woman, torn between loving two men—both pressing her for marriage.

I came back from lunch. The phone rang, and as my secretary answered it in the other office, I thought, *Lord, please, not for me.* It wasn't and I sighed.

It was then that I realized I needed to run. Fortunately, I could go then. I went nine miles, letting my mind soar into the sky. Cool breezes brushed my skin. Cumulus clouds swirled in the heavens above. Cars passed me, but I didn't really notice.

I know a place that's away from heavy traffic where I can run a course of anywhere from three to ten miles and seldom meet another person. As I ran, I thought of the story of Isaac. His servant had gone to seek a wife for him. The Bible says that Isaac walked in the field, meditating.

That's exactly how I felt: I meditated some, but mostly I just needed to be alone, away from people, away from telephones and voices. And I felt God's presence with me.

When I returned to the office, I was ready to tackle the problems with people again. I had been alone. Just the Lord and myself, away from everything for a time. Now I was ready to return to civilization and human needs.

Loving Lord, remind me that I need to get away from people, from noise, from pressures. I need to be alone with you. Amen.

Loving Me

"You must love the Lord your God with all your heart, all your soul, all your strength, and all your mind." And, "Love your neighbor as yourself." (Luke 10:27)

Week 5, Day 6

In the half-dozen books in my library on running (as well as two magazines on the sport I read), the aficionados continually remind us of the physical benefits from a regimen of jogging. They point out the obvious ones such as losing weight, lowering blood pressure, decreasing the risk of heart disease, improving digestion, and a lower incidence of all types of cancer.

What they don't stress enough is the less tangible benefit—and less measurable result—runners tend to feel better about themselves than their inactive counterparts. That is, we have learned that people who suffer from low self-esteem greatly improve their sense of self-worth from a routine of running.

In the 1970s Dr. Thaddeus Kostrubala, a San Diego psychiatrist, tried a new approach toward patients who appeared to make no progress. He began "running therapy," and his first group included a heroin addict, a suicide-prone person, and a manic-depressive. Later he reported that they had all made remarkable progress. He combined what he knew of psychiatric techniques with physical activity.

When I thought about it, it made sense. We are one person, and the body is an integral part of our being.

One man said, "Runners live longer—not that it necessarily gives them more years. But runners learn the value of life and improve the quality of it."

Count me as one of the disciples of this theory. Not that I had such a low self-image that I disliked myself. But I know that I enjoy life, appreciate nature, people, and myself more than ever before.

Sometimes, when running, I think of the goodness of God. I thank him that I can run and enjoy its pleasures. I thank him for the clear mind he has given me, for the talents I possess.

As I understand the New Testament, this is part of the great double commandment of Jesus. Jesus said first to love God totally and then love our neighbors in the same manner that we love ourselves. Only as we appreciate who we are and celebrate our individual uniqueness can we really appreciate other people.

In appreciating ourselves we also appreciate our bodies. I have more respect for this "wonderfully and fearfully made" body than ever before. In running, I become more sensitive to myself, my body, my inner system, and my relationship to my loving Creator.

How does this work out in a practical way? I used to believe that we should burn ourselves out for Jesus Christ. "Better to burn out than to rust out," went an old saying in the church. I almost burned out. Twice I ended up in the hospital with ulcers. That was the price of giving myself to Jesus and his service—or so I thought.

Once running hooked me, I learned to relax more. I still keep busy with many activities, but I've also learned to play a little more. Most of all, I like myself more than before.

As I understand myself and forgive myself, I also appreciate others. The better fit I am in the physical and spiritual, the more useful I become to God's kingdom.

Thanks, God, for loving me. And since you love me, I know it's okay for me to love myself, too. Amen.

WHAT MAKES
SAMMY RUN?

And later Isaiah spoke boldly for God, saying, "I was found by people who were not looking for me. I showed myself to those who were not asking for me." (Romans 10:20)

Week 5, Day 7

A generation ago, a best-selling novel titled *What Makes Sammy Run?* hit the stands. It concerned a young man on his way to the top. His attitude was seen in the way he moved—always in a run. And he didn't hesitate to knock over anyone along the way. He was running, and he was going to make it.

Perhaps for many of us, running along the roads fits in with our life-style—the man or woman who's aggressive and who's bound for the top.

Yet I've seen just as many (maybe even more) of the shy, introspective types who run. We may need to ask them the same question. Why do you run?

I started as part of a concern for physical fitness, because I thought it also went hand in hand with spiritual fitness. One friend began purely to lose weight. Another because he got tired of sitting in his office so many hours, and after running felt better.

I know runners who speak little about the physical differences because of their loping along the roads. They prefer to talk about their "highs" or their times of contemplation. Their eyes glow with the sense of God's presence as they move forward, often alone, usually in private communion with God.

What makes a runner run? There are no single answers. Those of us who run regularly and call ourselves committed to the sport run because we have to. We formed a habit, and then the habit formed us. We run because it meets needs we have—of privacy, of solitude, of breaking out of the norm; whatever the reason, we run. We can't *not* run.

It's that same kind of indescribable force that makes us follow after Jesus Christ. We pursue the knowledge of the Holy. It started, however, not with our pursuit. It started because God reached toward us.

The Apostle Paul says of God, "I have been found by those who did not seek me; I have shown myself to those who did not ask for me." God takes the initiative. He formed us with an urge to know him and to follow him. If we're true to ourselves, we run after God.

Lord Jesus, teach me to run after you always, and to hunger and thirst for a greater knowledge of you. Amen.

CHRISTIAN ADDICTION

I beseech you. . . (ye know the house of Stephanas, that it is the firstfruits of Achaia, and that they have addicted themselves to the ministry of the saints.) (1 Corinthians 16:15 KJV)

Week 6, Day 1

Stephanas must have been quite a man. In the King James Version, it reads that he and his household *addicted* themselves to helping God's people. That's positive addiction. None of the modern translations use the word because it has only a negative connotation.

And yet *positive* addiction is possible. Most of us have gotten the idea in the past few years that addiction destroys. We envision people acting compulsively and against their wills, weak individuals bound by habits and enslaved to them. We think of mainliners, who sell their bodies, possessions, and even their souls for a quick fix.

That's only one kind of addiction. Runners have a positive type. Their addiction comes upon them slowly. They start running for a variety of reasons, such as to improve health or lose weight. But once they get into it, the running becomes more than a habit; it's an addiction.

Runners actually make a narcotic within their own bodies, chemically similar to morphine. Runners speak of euphoric experiences or a "high" in regular, long running. People who run at least half an hour frequently report feeling an altered state of consciousness. Though the results are still coming in, it appears that for those who exercise vigorously the hypnotically repetitive rhythms cause this substance in the brain to release the hormone epinephrine. The hormone is the chemical basis for happy feelings.

On this matter of positive addiction, Dr. William Glasser wrote a book with that title in which he reported that running gives a wide range of emotional support, including increased self-confidence and ability to use the imagination, which in turn helps make life more enjoyable.

Thirty years ago *Psychology Today* magazine studied the effects of running on behavior. They concluded that people who began running tended to become more imaginative, self-sufficient, and emotionally stable, even when they had not been that way before.

Thinking about addiction makes me aware that I am addicted to running. That addiction may be one of the reasons I continue to enjoy running.

It also makes me aware of my need for positive addiction in all areas of my life. Most of all, I'd like to have the addiction of Stephanas. The Living

Bible paraphrases 1 Corinthians this way: "Do you remember Stephanas and his family? They were the first to become Christians in Greece and they are spending their lives helping and serving Christians everywhere."

Lord, make me a Christian addict—addicted to caring for others today...tomorrow...every day. Amen.

COMPETING WITH ME

*God has given us different gifts for doing certain things
well. (Romans 12:6)*

Week 6, Day 2

One reason running appeals to me is that it can
override competition. I'm not talking about
those who make top-grade runners in marathons or
the Olympics. I mean the common kind of runners I
see in the health spas and on the streets where I live.

I've participated in dozens of 5K and 10K runs. I
always give it my best. Yet I'm not competing against
anyone. I'm running for me. If there's any competition, it's against myself.

I wish all fun runs were really *fun* runs. In 1979
I ran in one large 10K race and hated it. I saw no
smiles. Everyone seemed bent on beating everyone
else. I stopped participating in the so-called "fun
runs." Then the following year my daughter encouraged me to run with her in a 10K race. I'm glad I did.

Less than a mile out, one fellow in red shorts and
orange tee shirt passed me. A few minutes later I over-
took him. A few minutes later, he breezed past me. Every

hill I charged ahead of him, but on the downgrade he took the lead. We laughed and waved at each other.

That's how I like to run. That's also how I like to go through life. My competitive spirit is there, but it's more internal than external. As a writer, I'm trying to be the best writer I can be. I'm not trying to be the best writer in the world (who knows who that person is anyway?), but I want to be the best I can with the amount of talent that God has given me.

My self-competition spreads through all parts of my life. For instance, in my level of discipleship I'm trying to live closer to Jesus Christ this year than I did last year and the year before that.

My self-competitive goals are not so much that I want to *do* more (more running or more writing), but that I want to *be* more.

Last year I set up a running goal of thirty miles a week. I just made it on the nose (and I skipped almost two weeks of running during the summer and had to really work at it to make my goal). This year I've set my goal for thirty-two miles a week. I'm competing against me—not against my wife or anyone else. I'm trying to sharpen my talents and my own gifts.

After all, that's all God really expects of us. He gives talents to whom he will, making some excel in one area, some in another. Our responsibility is to give our best with what we've got.

Holy Lord, you give each of us talents. Help me realize mine and then enable me to use them to glorify you and to serve others. Amen.

Runner's Joy

Always be full of joy in the Lord. I say it again—rejoice!
(Philippians 4:4)

Week 6, Day 3

A syndicated columnist lampooning runners said, "I hate runners because their feet smell and their faces are always so grim."

I laughed when I read the column. Afterward, I looked at pictures of runners in the magazines devoted to that sport. I've watched those who run the races. Sure enough, they have that grim set to their faces. Some of them show the pain they're going through. They breathe heavily, huffing and puffing as they move along.

"They're not a very happy lot, are they?" one woman said as we watched a TV replay of highlights of the Boston Marathon.

I wondered how she knew they weren't happy. Was she, like the columnist, basing that entirely on their faces during the race? I suppose so. But then, as I've watched pictures of football players charging across the filed or running for the goal, they're not smiling either. I've watched pictures of skiers, swimmers, and participants in practically every sport. I don't see smiles as they participate. They're busy concentrating. They're giving themselves, for the moment at least, entirely to the sport itself. It's when they reach the end of the game that the smiles appear.

Are runners unhappy because they don't smile? I don't think that's a fair question. It implies that all joy shows on our faces.

As I see it, joy is an attitude, a state of mind. It's a calmness in the face of hardship and adversity. Joy means facing life on the terms we find it, and with a confidence that we're going to make it through life with Jesus Christ right beside us all the way.

I can't picture Jesus smiling on the cross. I can't think of his grinning when he stood before Pilate. But I can picture him smiling when I pray. I can visualize a warm smile when he healed blind Bartimaeus. When walking along the road to Emmaus with his disciples, I see a hint of a smile.

The Book of Hebrews declares that ". . . Because of the joy awaiting [Jesus], he endured the cross. . . " (Hebrews 12:2). That's the real secret of joy. It's not the grueling ordeal of the moment that counts. It's what follows—the attitude after suffering, struggling, and pain.

When I see runners with determined jaws and glazed eyes, I know they're giving their all to the immediate task at hand—their running.

But look at them when they stop. They smile. They laugh. They're enjoying life at its fullest.

Jesus probably didn't smile at Calvary. But he knew a deep, inner joy because he knew what lay beyond the suffering. He knew that resurrection would follow. And so, for the joy that was set before him, he endured.

The example of Jesus stands before us. We rejoice, no matter what the present circumstances, because we know what lies ahead.

Lord Jesus, you knew joy by overcoming the cross. You've also made me your child so that I can rejoice. Remind me of that throughout the day. Amen.

THE VICTORIOUS

"To everyone who is victorious I will give fruit from the tree of life in the paradise of God." (Revelation 2:7)

Whoever is victorious will not be harmed by the second death. (Revelation 2:11)

Week 6, Day 4

Even with the hundreds of miles traveled on foot each year, I still hate hills. They're tough on me. They're not only harder to run on than flat surfaces, they slow down my overall speed. I can run six miles on an indoor track in nearly four minutes less than I can outdoors.

I dread hills, and for a long time I found ways not to fight them. But as I've done more running, I've also accepted the fact that hill running is part of the game. I use certain muscles on hills I don't use on the flat surface. Difficult hills demand more endurance. More than that, every time I reach the top of a difficult hill, I have a sense of well-being. I have conquered— perhaps only a quarter-mile incline, maybe a half mile of gradual upswing in the earth's path. But when I reach the top, I know I've struggled and I've overcome.

Two miles from my house looms a hill which all of us runners dread. It's steep and turns sharply twice. It took me weeks to reach the top without stopping to walk. Most runners I see attempting the ascent usually give up about halfway.

I make it regularly now, but I remember the first time I reached the top without slowing down. I felt as great as if I had won a marathon. I wanted to shout to the whole world, "I made it! I made it!"

So much of the Christian life works that way. We grow by facing obstacles. Not merely facing, but challenging them.

Sometimes those obstacles appear insurmountable. But we keep struggling and we make it… somehow.

When I ran my first race, a 5K (3.1 miles), I struggled against a steep hill, not sure if I could make it. I raised my eyes from my feet to the road ahead. Two women stood at the side, yelling and encouraging us. "Go on! You can make it!" they screamed.

As I got closer I cried out, "How much farther to the end?"

One of them laughed and yelled back, "As soon as you reach the top, turn right, and you run downhill about a hundred yards!"

Those words gave me the impetus I needed. New energy flowed through my body, and I charged the rest of the hill. And I made it. Yet, only seconds before I was ready to give up altogether.

I raced ahead, passing at least a dozen runners, enjoying every step of the way because I saw the finish line ahead.

Life often works that way. We keep on, sometimes wanting to give up. Many days we concentrate on simply placing one foot in front of the other. And during those times when we're not sure we can make it, Jesus Christ calls out encouraging words: "I am with you always." Then we know we can make it.

He holds rewards for us, encouraging us to continue. "To everyone who is victorious I will give fruit from the tree of life in the paradise of God. (Revelation 2:7)

King Jesus, encourage me today. Strengthen me to overcome the obstacles that face me. Amen.

COMING APART

Then Jesus said, "Let's go off by ourselves to a quiet place and rest awhile." He said this because there were so many people coming and going that Jesus and his apostles didn't even have time to eat. (Mark 6:31)

Week 6, Day 5

Bill Rogers, master runner of the 1970s who actually won the Boston Marathon four times, didn't win the 1976 event. In fact, he didn't even finish. Around the twentieth mile, he simply dropped out of the race.

Bill said in an interview he knew that if he continued, he could cause himself serious injury. While it might have caused his pride to buckle under a bit, he used wisdom. He knew that dropping out now would save him for later races. (He won the Boston Marathon again the following year.)

At times all of us need to drop out of the race, the race of actual running or the frenzied activities we find ourselves encumbered with. Now and then we all have to "come apart by yourselves...and rest a while," to use a paraphrase of the words of Jesus.

If we're sensitive to our bodies, and to the way God speaks through this wonderful human form, like Bill Rogers, we drop out for a short time. Even if we aren't that much in tune with our bodies, we have other ways of knowing when it's time to come aside and rest.

Once during my missionary days in Africa, my wife gently suggested that I slow down. My own body tried to tell me because I found myself weak and struggling against constant fatigue. I kept going. One day a missionary nurse with the Church of England, whom I scarcely knew, said, "You look and act like a man who needs to take a holiday."

I didn't listen. In those days I did not believe in "coming apart and resting." My condition got worse. One morning I could not get out of bed. I did not have the energy to pull myself out and rush into the day. I finally stayed in bed until midday, and then hobbled into the kitchen. I made myself breakfast and went back to sleep.

It actually took me months to get back to my full steam again. If I had listened to my body, my wife, and the nurse, I could have slowed down. Most of all, I didn't listen to God as he spoke through them.

I believe God tried to speak to me through my weakening condition. He built into our systems warning signs such as fatigue or loss of appetite. We operate at less than full efficiency when we've over-extended ourselves, when we've gone too long without rest, when we have stayed under constant strain.

As a result, our bodies develop a cold, a heart condition, ulcers, a sense of uselessness. And often the answer had been so simple, "Come apart by yourselves....and rest."

Lord Jesus, you understood the need to come apart and rest. I forget that lesson; so keep reminding me. Amen.

Turning Others On

"You are the light of the world—like a city on a hilltop that cannot be hidden. No one lights a lamp and then puts it under a basket. Instead, a lamp is placed on a stand, where it gives light to everyone in the house. In the same way, let your good deeds shine out for all to see, so that everyone will praise your heavenly Father." (Matthew 5:14–16)

Week 6, Day 6

Years ago, Shirley and I ran across uneven streets in the Mulberry Hill section of London. One woman, obviously waiting for a bus, called after us, "That's exactly what I should be doing!" and waved us on.

Two other people called out similar words as we trudged on. All of them were overweight and looked as though they needed a good exercise program.

Since my own conversion to running, I've tried to talk to people about getting in shape. I'm not such a devotee of running that I think it's the only sport. I'm quite willing to suggest that people might take up cycling or swimming. But I plead, take up *something*.

Surprisingly, people resist physical exercise. And they can offer excuses. I know. I went through years of offering reasons why I couldn't get my body into shape.

"I'm too busy now," I said. "If I take off an hour a day three times a week, that just leaves me further behind."

Another excuse: "I'm too tired now." How about this: "I'm not the athletic type." Someone always comes up with a specific case of "I knew a man once who exercised and...."

Aside from excuses, I actually tried exercises such as jogging and cycling, but neither attempt lasted more than a few days. Calisthenics went on for ten days before boredom set in.

Then it seemed as if everyone I knew either had started to run or talked about it. Articles in newspapers and magazines appeared before me. TV newscasts featured clips of races among other sports events. Eventually I decided to run—and to make it a serious commitment.

I've stayed at running and keeping in shape. I now weigh less than I did at the time of my military discharge at age twenty-two.

And because I believe in exercise, I talk about it to others. When even hints come their way about getting into shape, they have a bag filled with excuses. I've probably heard them all by now. Often I've tried to argue or persuade people to stop excusing their inactivity and get into shape.

The other day it occurred to me that getting people into a shape-up program is similar to turning people to Jesus Christ.

Persuasive nagging seldom has a lasting effect on people. Logical arguments usually get a nod and a smile, but no action.

I decided that the best argument for physical fitness is *example*. I run and love it. I'm not a six-month devotee who has quit after a trial period. I make space in my week for running.

Not that I have brought a thousand people into physical-fitness programs, but personal example works best. I've lost weight. My blood pressure which once sneaked into the danger range now stays in the comfortable safe level. My heart beats slower (and the doctors tell me I ought to live longer). I feel better about myself and about life.

From the words of Jesus I see this same message. He told us to let our lights shine before people, so they could see the good things in us that glorify the Father.

He also said that if we have something special in life, it shows. We don't have to force it on people. We don't have to hammer away at them. They can see if we are different, and they know the positive changes we've made.

I still like talking about running (and most of us devotees of the sport do), but more and more I'm learning to let my example speak.

The best way to turn another person on is to turn on myself.

Lord God, turn me on. Then let my life excite others. Amen.

GETTING RID OF HOLES

"For God loved the world so much that he gave his one and only Son, so that everyone who believes in him will not perish but have eternal life. God sent his Son into the world not to judge the world, but to save the world through him." (John 3:16–17)

Week 6, Day 7

I don't remember much about my second-grade curriculum, but I recall a crazy story we read about an old woman. One day she discovered to her horror that her favorite blanket was filled with small holes. She fretted for half a page and then hit upon a solution. She grabbed a pair of scissors to cut out the holes. Even in second grade, I appreciated the absurd humor of the story.

Yet sometimes people get caught up in trying to cut out holes in all kinds of ways. For instance, one area of physical exercise I've read about lately involves spot reducing. Books fill the marketplace with detailed exercise programs and a variety of vitamin supplements to remove fat from certain spots. The trouble is, spot reducing proves as futile as getting rid of holes by cutting them out.

We can't lose fat from a particular part of the body just by exercising. For example, one book tells me that I can get rid of fat in my tummy area by performing twenty sit-ups daily. Twenty daily sit-ups will strengthen and tighten up my stomach muscles. They won't remove fat from the belly.

Many studies have come out showing us that the way to lose fat from the body comes about in only one way: Burn more calories than you take in. The average person must burn at least 300 calories in a half-hour workout and do this at least three times a week.

Another fallacy of cutting out holes centers on trying to be good. We've often gotten the idea that if we behave, don't do anything particularly bad, we're all right and God will have to love us. That's backward theology.

The real message is that God loves us, and when we respond to his love and surrender to Jesus Christ, then we'll want to be good. This makes our attempt to be good the *result* of a relationship with a loving Heavenly Father. The backward theology involves trying to earn salvation from God. And when we try to earn his favor, we're cutting out the holes.

As I remember the story about the old woman, she finally hit upon a practical solution. She cut her blanket into small pieces and made winter coats for her ducks.

Recalling that story reminds me of the sign I see occasionally: GOD DON'T MAKE NO JUNK. That's one of the ways to tell us that no human is beyond the touch of God's love. Even the most debased person is still of great value to our loving Jesus Christ.

Loving Lord, of all the billions of people in the world's history, I am just one. But I am one who is loved by you. Thanks, Lord, and don't let me ever forget. Amen.

Running Hints

1. "Train, don't strain." Don't overdo it, especially when you first start.
2. Don't be afraid to walk. Run your course; but if you're overexerting yourself, listen to your body. Slow down.
3. If you're just getting started, *aim* for thirty minutes, three times a week. Don't try to reach that level too quickly. Build up to it over a period of weeks, even months.
4. Commit yourself into getting into shape. Remember, God wants your body at its best.
5. Make running a long-term commitment. Determine to continue at least one year.
6. If you have any questions about your physical condition, consult a physician before you start a running program. Don't ask if you *should* run, but if you *can* run.
7. Running is a natural tranquilizer.
8. Running, combined with sensible diet, is an excellent way to lose weight.

9. Running can be one of the most significant experiences in your life. It's usually not fun in the beginning, but stick with it.

10. The secret of a good running form is to run naturally. Keep your body straight, your head up, and lean slightly forward. Run with your elbows bent but not held tightly against your chest. Don't run on your toes! Strike the ground at the heel and roll forward.

11. Especially in the beginning, forget about speed. You're running for yourself, not to compete with someone else's time.

12. The first time you run, don't attempt more than half a mile. You may have to settle for 200 yards.

13. When you first start running, you'll probably get sore legs. If you have severe pain, you're pushing too hard or too long. Soreness is your body's way to tell you that you're getting back into shape.

14. Don't worry about setbacks. If you miss a few days, forgive yourself and start over again.

15. From the beginning, make running a habit. Set aside a time solely for running, with enough time for changing, warming up, and cooling down.

Extra Running Hints

1. The harder, longer, or faster you run the greater your benefits—to a point. Paying attention to your body will help you not to overdo.
2. Studies now show that running or walking uphill burns almost 30 percent more calories than cycling.
3. Running on a treadmill produces the same benefits of running outside. Although I prefer outdoor running, the treadmill seems easier on the body
4. Logically, walking or running the same distance should burn the same calories. But studies show that the *intensity* of running burns about 30 percent more calories than jogging.
5. One benefit of running is that no matter where I go, running shoes, tee shirt, and shorts are all I need. For those of us who travel by air, running, jogging, or walking puts our equipment into our luggage with little extra weight.

DEVOTIONS FOR DIETERS

IGNORANCE PAYS

Regarding your question about the special abilities the Spirit gives us. I don't want you to misunderstand this. (1 Corinthians 12:1)

In my mid-thirties I became aware of my increased weight. "I'll have to do something about it," I said to myself and my wife several times.

Then I took the plunge and started out. Over the years I had accumulated incorrect information such as: proteins help you lose weight and carbohydrates make you gain. For the next week I loaded up on protein—eating meat almost exclusively, and lots of it. I particularly liked salami, polish sausage, and pork chops. Somehow that idea didn't work. I actually put on two pounds.

I tried cutting out desserts and eliminating sugar and milk in my coffee. However, a little marmalade on my toast didn't count much. Ice milk wasn't as fattening as ice cream. I kept gaining.

It took a few more years and frustrated dieting before I realized a stark truth: ignorance pays the wrong kind of dividends.

Like a lot of people who wanted to drop off the pounds, I went about it the wrong way. It was only when I learned about nutrition and sensible calorie counting that the excess baggage started disappearing.

The Apostle Paul understood about ignorance. He wrote to the Corinthian church about that very subject. They had been a greatly blessed church—he said in the first chapter that they lacked nothing in spiritual gifts. But the apostle had a lot of straightening out to do with that local congregation. In chapters 12–14 he wrote about the meaning, purpose, and use of these gifts. But he prefaced his remarks with these words: "Now concerning spiritual gifts, brethren, I do not want you to be uninformed."

Because they had been ignorant, they had all kinds of confusion in that congregation. He wrote to enlighten them and set them straight.

Knowing we need to lose weight, plus a few isolated facts, aren't enough. We need to learn about nutrition. We need to learn how our body operates. As we learn more, we not only rid ourselves of misinformation, but we learn how to slim down and live with a body that's healthier and happier.

Great Teacher, help me learn about calories and losing weight. Don't let me foolishly do all the wrong things in a misguided attempt to drop off pounds. Amen.

FACING MYSELF

But don't just listen to God's word. You must do what it says. Otherwise, you are only fooling yourselves. For if you listen to the word and don't obey, it is like glancing at your face in a mirror. You see yourself, walk away, and forget what you look like. (James 1:22–24)

I'll never forget the day that I made my decision to count calories. I had come out of the shower, and standing in the bathroom I saw a side view of myself. I didn't like what I saw: a paunchy stomach, flabby arms, thickening thighs, a collar size a full inch bigger than it had ever been before in my life. That's when I decided to do something about it. And I did! I determined that day I would begin to count calories and would not stop until I had lost at least twenty-five pounds.

That may not sound like a lot of weight for some people to lose, but every pound is hard to lose. It meant not only a commitment to counting calories, a strict discipline, but it also entailed at least two other things.

First, I had to be *honest* with God and myself. I wanted to lose weight. I determined to become a trim person, even when old habits kept attacking me. I often prayed, "Lord, help me stick to my diet, even when I don't want to."

The other thing is, I knew I would fail once in a while. I had to learn to forgive myself. Forgiving myself meant saying to God and to Cec, "Okay, you blew it. Do better next time."

I learned that I couldn't just see that I needed to lose weight, I had to do something about it. By acting on my concern, I became the kind of person the Apostle James commends when he says it isn't enough to hear God's Word. We must also obey it. Those who only hear are like people who see themselves in a mirror and then forget what they look like. I had seen my flabby self many times and quickly erased the visual image. But the day I started to count calories I not only saw my image; I determined to change it. With God's help I have done that.

Lord Jesus, thank you for showing me myself. Help me to remember what I look like and give me a vision of what I can be. Amen.

SECRET SINS

You spread out our sins before you—our secret sins—and you see them all. (Psalm 90:8)

A health spa sign proclaimed, WHAT YOU EAT IN PRIVATE SHOWS UP IN PUBLIC. Next to the sign stood the scales. For me this graphically illustrates that we get away with nothing. Some people on diets seem to think that a tiny cookie, an extra spoonful of mashed potatoes and gravy, or only a small piece of cake won't count; no one will know. But we never really get away with anything. Still we keep trying to deceive others and ourselves.

Sometimes I've watched people eat forbidden food or extra amounts, discount it with a smile and say, "I'll have to run around the block a couple of extra times." I don't think they ever run around the block a couple of extra times. Even if they did, that wouldn't make up for the overindulgence.

We all get caught in the secret sin syndrome. Sometimes we think we can do something wrong—a sin which isn't very bad—and it won't count. Or later we can ask God to forgive us and no one

121

will know. But no sin is ever secret, because God knows.

We need to remind ourselves that when we count calories we're not only helping our bodies; we're also trying to please God, and we don't please him by cheating.

Lord God, as a calorie counter help me to be honest with you and with myself, in public or in secret. Amen.

About the Author

New York Times bestselling author Cecil (Cec) Murphey has written or co-written more than 135 books, including the bestsellers *90 Minutes in Heaven* (with Don Piper) and *Gifted Hands: The Ben Carson Story* (with Dr. Ben Carson). His books have sold in the millions and have brought hope and encouragement to countless people around the world.

Visit his website at www.CecilMurphey.com and follow him on Twitter at www.Twitter.com/CecMurphey.

www.ingramcontent.com/pod-product-compliance
Lightning Source LLC
Chambersburg PA
CBHW020548030426
42337CB00013B/1010